Amusement Park
Word Problems Starring
Pre-Algebra

Rebecca

Wingard-Nelson

Enslow Elementary, an imprint of Enslow Publishers, Inc.

Enslow Elementary® is a registered trademark of Enslow Publishers, Inc.

Library of Congress Cataloging-in-Publication Data

Wingard-Nelson, Rebecca.
  Amusement park word problems starring pre-algebra : math word problems solved / Rebecca Wingard-Nelson.
      p. cm.— (Math word problems solved)
  Includes bibliographical references and index.
  Summary: "Explores methods of solving pre-algebra word problems using amusement park examples"—Provided by publisher.
  ISBN-13: 978-0-7660-2922-4
  ISBN-10: 0-7660-2922-0
  1. Algebra—Juvenile literature. 2. Word problems (Mathematics)—Juvenile literature. 3. Amusement parks—Juvenile literature. I. Title.
QA155.15.W564 2009
  512.0076—dc22
                                    2008030787

Printed in the United States of America

10 9 8 7 6 5 4 3 2 1

To Our Readers: We have done our best to make sure all Internet Addresses in this book were active and appropriate when we went to press. However, the author and the publisher have no control over and assume no liability for the material available on those Internet sites or on other Web sites they may link to. Any comments or suggestions can be sent by e-mail to comments@enslow.com or to the address on the back cover.

♻ Enslow Publishers, Inc., is committed to printing our books on recycled paper. The paper in every book contains 10% to 30% post-consumer waste (PCW). The cover board on the outside of each book contains 100% PCW. Our goal is to do our part to help young people and the environment too!

Illustrations: Tom LaBaff

Cover illustration: Tom LaBaff

Free Worksheets are available for this book at http://www.enslow.com. Search for the **Math Word Problems Solved** series name. The publisher will provide access to the worksheets for five years from the book's first publication date.

Contents

Introduction

"Why do I have to do math?"

Math is used in your life every day.

Word problems show you some of the ways.

"But I hate word problems."

You use word problems all the time, and you probably don't even realize it.

"The stories in word problems would never happen!"

Sometimes math word problems don't look very real. A lot of real-life word problems are very hard to solve. For now, have fun getting started on word problems about amusement parks.

"How can this book help me?"

This book will give you helpful tips for solving a word problem. Learn how to understand the question, how to plan a way to solve it, and how to check your answer. You'll see that word problems really are "no problem" after all!

Problem-Solving Tips

Word problems might be part of your homework, on a test, or in your life. These tips can help you solve them, no matter where they show up.

 ### Be positive!
When you get a problem right the first time, good for you! When you don't get a problem right the first time, but you learn from your mistakes, AWESOME for you! You learned something new!

 ### Get help early!
New problems build on old ones. If you don't understand today's problem, tomorrow's problem will be even harder to understand.

 ### Do your homework!
The more you practice anything, the better you become at it. You can't play an instrument or play a sport well without practice. Homework problems are your practice.

Move on!
If you get stuck, move on to the next problem. Do the ones you know how to solve first. You'll feel more confident. And you won't miss the ones you know because you ran out of time. Go back later and try the problems you skipped.

Ask questions!

When someone is helping you, asking good questions tells the person what you don't understand. If you don't ask questions, you will never get answers!

Take a break!

If you have tried everything you can think of but are only getting frustrated, take a break. Close your eyes and take a deep breath. Stretch your arms and legs. Get a drink of water or a snack. Then come back and try again.

Don't give up!

The first time you try to solve a word problem, you might come up with an answer that does not make sense, or that you know is not right. Don't give up! Check your math. Try solving the problem a different way. If you quit, you won't learn.

In some problems, you will see clue spotters. A magnifying glass will help you spy clue words in the problem.

Problem-Solving Steps

Word problems can be solved by following four easy steps.

Here's the problem.

The greatest speed of the fastest steel roller coaster is 134 mph. The greatest speed of the fastest wooden roller coaster is 78 mph. How much faster is the steel roller coaster's greatest speed?

Read and understand the problem.
Read the problem carefully.
Ask yourself questions, such as:

What do you know?
The greatest speed of the fastest steel roller coaster is 134 mph.
The greatest speed of the fastest wooden roller coaster is 78 mph.

What are you trying to find?
How much faster the steel roller coaster is than the wooden roller coaster.

What kind of problem is this?
You want to know the difference between the two greatest speeds. Problems that find a difference are subtraction problems.

Make a plan.

Some problems tell you how they should be solved. They may say "draw a picture" or "write an equation." For other problems, you will need to make your own plan. Most problems can be solved in more than one way. Some plans you might try are:

Look for a pattern   Write an equation
Draw a picture   Use a model
Estimate   Break it apart

How can you solve this problem?
Let's write an equation.

Pattern?

estimate?   equation?

Picture?   model?

break it apart?

9

Solve the problem.

It is time to do the math!
If you find that your plan
is not working, make a new
plan. Don't give up the first time.

Let's write an equation.
Use the numbers from the problem to write a
subtraction equation.

Start with the greatest speed of the steel roller
coaster, 134 mph. Subtract the greatest speed of
the wooden roller coaster, 78 mph, to find the
difference.

$134 - 78 = 56$

**The greatest speed of the steel roller coaster
is 56 mph faster than the greatest speed of
the wooden roller coaster.**

Look back.

The problem is solved!
But you aren't finished yet.
Take a good look at your answer.
Does it make sense? Did you include the units?
Did you use the right numbers to begin? Estimate
or use a different operation to check your math.

Did you answer the right question? Yes.

Is there another way you can solve this problem?
Yes. You could use a number line to find the
difference between 78 and 134. Count the number
of places betwen 78 and 134.

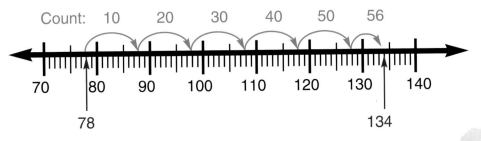

Count: 10   20   30   40   50   56

70   80   90   100   110   120   130   140

78   134

Clue Words

Clue words can help you figure out how to solve problems.

Here's the problem.

In one amusement park, 21 of the rides are water rides and 16 are not water rides. How many rides are there combined?

Addition

Problems that combine values, such as rides, are addition problems.

In this problem the clue word "combined" tells you to add the water rides and the non-water rides. Some other clue words that tell you a problem might use addition are: add, sum, total, plus, more, together, increase, and both.

Here's the problem.

At one amusement park, 21 of the rides are water rides and 16 rides are not water rides. How many more rides are water rides than non-water rides?

SUBTRACTION

Subtraction

Problems that find the difference between two values, such as rides, are subtraction problems. Problems that start with a value and then take some away also use subtraction.

In this problem the clue words "how many more" tell you to find the difference between the number of water rides and the number of non-water rides. Some other clue words that tell you a problem might use subtraction are: subtract, difference, take away, how much less, how much farther, remain, left, fewer, and compare.

Each ride on the Ferris wheel takes 3 tickets. If 6 people want to ride the Ferris wheel together, how many tickets do they need?

Multiplication

Problems that tell you a quantity for one item and ask you to find a quantity for more than one item are multiplication problems.

In this problem, the clue word "each" tells you that you know the quantity of tickets for one ride, 3. You need to find the quantity of tickets for 6 rides. This is a multiplication problem. Some other clue words that tell you a problem might use multiplication are: at, every, multiply, of, per, product, rate, times, and twice.

A family of 6 people used 18 tickets to ride the Ferris wheel once. How many tickets does the Ferris wheel cost per ride?

Division

Problems that tell you a quantity for more than one item and ask you to find a quantity for one item are division problems.

You are given the number of tickets (18) for 6 people to ride. The clue word "per" tells you to find the number of tickets for one person to ride. This is division. Some other clue words that tell you a problem might use division are: divided, each, equally, evenly, every, half, and split.

Opposite Problems

Let's look at the facts from the Ferris wheel problems.

Each ride takes 3 tickets. Six people want to ride. Six rides take 18 tickets.

Using these facts, you can write two types of problems.

Multiplication:

6 rides × 3 tickets each = 18 tickets

Division:

18 tickets ÷ 6 rides = 3 tickets each

Because they are related, operations that are the opposite sometimes use the same clue words, such as "per" and "each." The clue words will help you get started, but you must understand what is happening in the problem, and what question is being asked.

More Than One Operation

The order of operations is a set of rules that tells you the order in which to perform operations, such as addition or multiplication.

Here's the problem.

The Cleaver family found a food stand that sold whole pizzas and pizza by the slice. They bought 2 whole pizzas that contained 4 slices each and another slice by itself. How many slices of pizza did they buy in all?

MULTIPLICATION

ADDITION

Read and understand.

What do you know?
The Cleavers bought 2 whole pizzas with 4 slices in each pizza. They also bought 1 single slice.

What are you trying to find?
The number of slices the Cleavers bought in all.

Plan.

Let's write an equation.

Solve.

Write an equation to
match the problem.
Let's write it in words first.

number of pizzas	times	slices in each pizza	plus	one more slice	equals	slices in all
2	×	4	+	1	=	slices in all

The order of operations tells you to multiply first,
then add.

Multiply first. 2 pizzas × 4 slices each = 8 slices.

Then add. 8 slices + 1 more slice = 9 slices in all.

The Cleavers bought 9 slices of pizza in all.

Look back.

*Does the order of operations make sense with the
problem?* Yes. You must find the number of slices in
the two pizzas before you add the extra piece.

What happens if you add before you multiply?
Use parentheses around the addition part to show
you want to add first. To solve $2 \times (4 + 1)$, first add
inside the parentheses. $4 + 1 = 5$. Then multiply.
$2 \times 5 = 10$. The equation $2 \times (4 + 1) = 10$ does not
equal $2 \times 4 + 1 = 9$.

17

Draw a Picture

You can draw a picture to see that you can multiply numbers in any order and the answers will be the same. You can also add numbers in any order and the answers will be the same.

Here's the problem.

Sonya won a stuffed snake at the balloon game. The game board had 10 rows of balloons with 16 balloons in each row. How many balloons were on the game board?

MULTIPLICATION

Read and understand.

What do you know?
The game board had 10 rows of balloons with 16 balloons in each row.

What are you trying to find?
The number of balloons on the game board.

Plan.

Let's draw a picture.

Solve.

Draw a simple picture. Represent each balloon with an X. There are 10 rows with 16 in each row.

10

16

To find the total number of balloons, you can count each X, you can add the Xs in each row (16 + 16 . . .), or you can multiply 10 rows × 16 in each row.

10 × 16 = 160

There were 160 balloons on the game board.

Look back.

Does it matter if you multiply 10 × 16 or 16 × 10? No. In multiplication, the order of the factors does not matter. You can use the picture to see that this is true. If you turn your picture sideways so there are 16 rows with 10 in each row, does the total change? No.

16

10

Mental Math

In an addition problem, you can group the numbers to make them easier to add in your head.

Here's the problem.

Anton rode the Gravitron 5 times by himself, 16 times with his friends, plus 4 more times with his little sister. How many times did he ride in all?

Read and understand.

What do you know?

Anton rode the Gravitron: 5 times alone
16 times with friends
4 times with his sister

What are you trying to find?

The number of times Anton rode the Gravitron in all.

Plan.

Let's use mental math.

> The Gravitron spins fast enough to push riders against the inside walls.
>
> It uses the same force you feel when you are riding in a car that goes quickly around a bend in the road.

Solve.

There are three numbers to add: 5 + 16 + 4

You can group the numbers to make them easier to add in your head.

Think: 5 + 16 + 4   16 + 4 = 20

Think: 5 +   20   5 + 20 = 25

Anton rode the Gravitron 25 times in all.

Look back.

Is the math correct? Use a paper and pencil to check the math. This time, add from left to right.

5 + 16 + 4   21 + 4 = 25 ✓
   21

Hidden Information

Hidden information is something you are not given directly in the problem but that you must know in order to solve it.

Here's the problem.

Sabrina rode on the log flume 8 times. She stayed dry on 0 of her log flume rides. On how many of her log flume rides did Sabrina get wet?

Read and understand.
What do you know?
Sabrina rode the log flume 8 times.
She stayed dry on 0 of her log flume rides.

What are you trying to find?
The number of rides that got Sabrina wet.

What hidden information is in the problem?
In this problem, you must know that wet and dry are opposites. Sabrina either stayed dry or got wet.

What kind of problem is this? There is no clue word, so decide what happens in the problem. Sabrina had a total of 8 log flume rides. She stayed dry on none of the rides. You want to find the remaining number of rides (the ones on which she did not stay dry). This is a subtraction problem.

Plan.
Let's write an equation.

22

Solve.

Use the numbers from the problem to write a subtraction equation.

Total rides – dry rides = wet rides

8 – 0 = 8

Sabrina got wet on 8 of her log flume rides.

> The math is easy when one of the numbers is zero.
>
> Adding or subtracting zero does not change a number.
>
> Multiplying by zero always results in zero.

Look back.

Check your subtraction by using addition.
Add the answer (8) to the number you subtracted (0).
If the sum (8) is the number you started with,
then your answer is correct. 8 + 0 = 8
Did you start with 8? Yes. ✔

Too Much Information

Some problems give more information than you need.

Here's the problem.

Bridget won 6 goldfish by throwing little balls into fishbowls. She paid $1.00 per ball for 12 balls. How much did Bridget spend at the fishbowl game?

Read and understand.

What do you know?
Bridget won 6 goldfish. She paid to throw 12 balls. Each ball cost $1.00.

What are you trying to find?
The amount of money Bridget spent at the fishbowl game.

What do you need to know to solve the problem?
How many balls she paid for, and how much she paid for each one. You do not need to know that she won 6 goldfish.

Are there any clue words?
Yes. The clue word "per" tells you this is multiplication or division. You know the cost of one ball ($1.00). You want to find the cost of more than one ball (12). This is multiplication.

 Plan.

Let's use what we know about ones.

 Solve.

When you multiply or divide any number by 1, the number stays the same.

The cost of one ball is $1.00, or $1, so the cost of 12 balls is 12 × 1, or $12.00.

Bridget spent $12.00 at the fishbowl game.

 Look back.

Could you have solved this problem another way?
You could draw a picture.
Draw 12 circles for the balls
Bridget paid for. Write $1
on each ball for the cost.
Now count the number of dollars. There are 12.

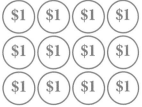

Find a Pattern

Tables can help you find patterns and solve problems.

Here's the problem.

Adrian's mom waved to him every time he passed her as he rode the carousel. After one ride, he passed her 12 times. After two rides, he passed her 24 times. Adrian took 6 rides on the carousel. How many times did he pass his mom?

Read and understand.

What do you know?
After 1 ride, Adrian passed his mom 12 times.
After 2 rides, he passed her 24 times.
Adrian rode the carousel 6 times.

What are you trying to find?
The number of times Adrian passed his mom.

Plan.

Let's make a table.

Solve.

Make a table that organizes what you know.
A table can make it easier to see a pattern.

number of rides	1	2	3	4	5	6
number of times past mom	12	24	36	48	60	72

(×12 between each column)

For each ride, Adrian passed his mom 12 times.
To find the total number of times he passed her,
you can add 12 more passes for each ride, or you
can multiply the number of rides by 12.

6 × 12 = 72

Adrian passed his mom 72 times.

Look back.

Does the answer match the question? Yes.
Did you include the units in the answer? Yes.

27

Write an Expression

Expressions can be numbers or a combination of numbers and operations. Expressions do not use the equal sign.

Here's the problem.

Hans stood in line for 14 minutes to ride the pirate ship. His ride was 6 minutes long. Write an expression that shows how to find the difference in minutes between Hans' time in line and his time on the ride.

Read and understand.

What do you know?
Hans stood in line for 14 minutes.
His ride lasted 6 minutes.

What are you trying to find?
An expression that shows how to find the difference in minutes between the time in line and the time on the ride.

Are there any clue words?
Yes. The word "difference" tells you this is a subtraction problem.

Plan.
Let's write an expression.

28

Solve.

Start with the number of minutes Hans stood in line, 14. Write the subtraction sign to show you must subtract. Then write the number of minutes Hans rode on the pirate ship, 6.

$$14 - 6$$

The expression that shows how to find the difference between Hans' time in line and his time on the ride is 14 – 6.

 Look back.

Did you answer the right question? Yes

Hans spent 8 minutes longer in line than he did on the ride. Why is 8 minutes the wrong answer? The problem does *not* ask you for the difference. It asks you to *write an expression* that shows how to find the difference. The answer 8 minutes does not show that you use subtraction.

29

Variable Expressions

You can use a letter or symbol in an expression to represent a number you don't know. The letter or symbol is called a variable.

Here's the problem.

Passes to an amusement park cost $39.75 each. Write an expression to show the cost of a number of passes. Use the letter *p* to represent the number of passes.

MULTIPLICATION

Many amusement parks charge one price to use all of the attractions.

In 1897, the first pass at a pay-one-price amusement park was sold for 25¢.

Read and understand.

What do you know?
The cost of one pass is $39.75.

What are you trying to find?
An expression that shows the cost of a number of passes.

Are there any clue words in the problem?
Yes. The clue word "each" tells you this is either a multiplication or division problem. The problem gives you the cost of one, and you need to show the cost of a number of passes. This is a multiplication problem.

Plan.

Let's write an expression.

Solve.

To find the cost of any number of passes, multiply the cost of one pass by the number of passes.

Cost of one pass times number of passes

$$\$39.75 \quad \times \quad p$$

An expression for the cost of a number of passes is $39.75 × p.

Look back.

Is there another way to write the expression?
Yes. You can write a multiplication expression without the multiplication sign. $39.75 × p$ can be written as $39.75p$.

More Than One Question

Problems with more than one question must have more than one answer.

? Here's the problem.

Nhu went down the giant slide 6 times, got a drink, then went down the slide some more times. Write an expression for how many times Nhu went down the slide in all. Then find the total number of times she went down the slide if she went down 10 more times after her drink.

Read and understand.

What do you know?
Nhu went down the giant slide 6 times, then she went down some more times.

What are you trying to find?
Two things: an **expression** for the total number of times Nhu went down the slide, and the **total** number of times if she went down the slide 10 times after her drink.

Plan.

Let's write the expression, then use the expression to find the answer.

Use the letter *s* to stand for the number of times Nhu went down the slide after she had a drink.

First Nhu went down   Then she went
   the slide 6 times.   down more times.

        6   +   s

**Nhu went down the
slide 6 + s times in all.**

If Nhu went down the slide
10 times after her drink, put   6 + s
10 into the expression in   6 + 10
place of the *s*. Then add.   16

**Nhu went down the slide
16 times in all.**

Look back.

*If Nhu went down the slide
6 times after her drink,
would the answer change?*
The expression (6 + s) would
be the same, but the total
would be different
(6 + 6 = 12).

Related Equations

An equation has an equal sign, but an expression does not.

Here's the problem.

There are 64 people riding in the bumper cars. Each car has 2 riders. There are 32 cars. Write a division equation that matches this problem, then write a related multiplication equation.

Read and understand.

What do you know?
There are 64 people riding in the bumper cars.
Each car has 2 riders. There are 32 cars.

What are you trying to find?
Two equations, one division and one multiplication.

Plan.

Let's write the equations.

Solve.

The problem tells you the total (64 riders), the number in each group (2 in a car), and the number of groups (32 cars). Write the division equation that matches the problem.

total riders ÷ riders in one car = number of cars
    64   ÷   2   =   32

One possible division equation is 64 ÷ 2 = 32.

Now write a related multiplication equation.

riders in car × number of cars = total riders
    2   ×   32   =   64

**A related multiplication equation is
2 × 32 = 64.**

Look back.

Did you answer the right question? Yes. The problem asked for two equations, a division equation and a related multiplication equation.

Solution Equations

Related equations can help you solve word problems.

Here's the problem.

? **Two people can ride in a waterslide raft together if they weigh less than 225 pounds total. Doug, who weighs 115 pounds, got into a raft. Eric got into the raft with Doug. Together, they weighed 220 pounds. How much does Eric weigh?** ?

ADDITION

 Read and understand.
What do you know?
Doug weighs 115 pounds.
Together, Doug and Eric weigh 220 pounds.

What are you trying to find?
Eric's weight.

Are there any clue words?
Yes. The word "together" shows addition is happening.

Plan.
Let's write an equation.

Solve.

Equations that match what happens in a problem are sometimes called situation equations. Write a situation equation for the problem.

Doug's weight + Eric's weight = weight together

$$115 \quad + \quad w \quad = \quad 220$$

Equations that are related to a situation equation, but are easier to solve, are sometimes called solution equations. Write a related solution equation that has the letter by itself on one side of the equal sign.

$115 + w = 220$ is related to $w = 220 - 115$

Now solve the related equation by subtracting.
$105 = 220 - 115$, so $w = 105$.

Eric weighs 105 pounds.

Look back.
Check your answer.
Put your answer, 105, into the original situation equation, then add.
$115 + 105 = 220$. The answer is correct. ✔

Pictures and Equations

A picture or diagram can help you write or solve equations.

Here's the problem.

In one mirror maze, there are 84 walls. Some of the walls are mirrored glass. The remaining 22 walls are clear glass. How many mirrored glass walls are there?

SUBTRACTION

Read and understand.

What do you know?

There are 84 walls in all.

Some of the walls are mirrored glass.

There are 22 walls of clear glass.

What are you trying to find?
The number of mirrored glass walls.

Plan.

Let's write an equation.

Solve.

The problem gives the number of total walls and clear walls. You do not know the number of mirrored walls. Use the letter m for the number you do not know.

total walls – mirrored walls = clear walls
$$84 \quad - \quad m \quad = \quad 22$$

To solve this equation, let's make a place-value drawing.

Start with 84 to represent the total walls.

84

Cross off values until there are only 22 remaining. What value did you cross off? 62.

22

There are 62 mirrored walls.

Look back.

Is there another way you could solve this problem?
Yes. You could solve the equation, $84 - m = 22$, by using the related equation $84 = 22 + m$, or $84 - 22 = m$. $84 - 22 = 62$, so $m = 62$.

Keep It Equal

You can do the same thing to each side of an equation, and the sides remain equal.

Here's the problem.

You must be at least 54 inches tall to ride the Tilt-A-Whirl without an adult. Jenna needs to grow another 3 inches before she can do this. How tall is Jenna now?

Read and understand.
What do you know?
You must be 54 inches tall to ride without an adult. Jenna needs to grow 3 inches to ride without an adult.

What are you trying to find?
Jenna's height now.

Plan.
Let's write an equation.

Solve.
Write a situation equation to match the problem.

Jenna's height + 3 inches = height to ride alone
$$h + 3 = 54$$

You can find an unknown value in an equation by getting the unknown by itself on one side of the equal sign. One way to get the unknown by itself is to do the same operation on each side of an equation.

To get h alone, you can subtract 3 from each side.
$$h + 3 = 54$$
$$h + 3 - 3 = 54 - 3$$
$$h + 0 = 51$$
$$h = 51$$

Jenna is 51 inches tall.

Look back.
Check your math. Put the answer (51) into the original equation ($h + 3 = 54$). $51 + 3 = 54$ ✓

Use a Formula

A formula is a special equation that uses letters to stand for values.

A wave pool has waves that are like ocean waves, but the beach part is made of concrete.

Here's the problem.

The wave pool is a square pool with a side length of 200 feet. Dai walked the whole way around the wave pool one time. How far did he walk? Use the formula for the perimeter of a square ($P = 4s$).

15'

Read and understand.

What do you know?

The wave pool is a square. Each side is 200 feet long. Dai walked around the pool one time.

What are you trying to find?
How far Dai walked.

How are you told to solve the problem?
Use the formula for the perimeter of a square.

Plan.

Let's use the formula.

Solve.

Write the formula. In this formula, *P* stands for perimeter, or distance around. The letter *s* stands for the length of one side.

$$P = 4s$$

Put the numbers you know from the problem into the formula. You know the side length is 200 feet.

$$P = 4 \times 200 \quad \text{Multiply.} \quad 4 \times 200 = 800$$
$$P = 800$$

Dai walked 800 feet.

Look back.

Check the answer.
Since multiplication is repeated addition, you can add the length for each side.
200 + 200 + 200 + 200 = 800. ✓

43

Logical Reasoning

Some problems cannot be solved using arithmetic. You need to use only your thinking skills.

Here's the problem.

Liza, Juno, and Tessa are waiting in line for the chair swing. Liza is directly in front of Juno. Ashe cuts in line directly in front of Tessa. Tessa is somewhere behind Liza. Of the four friends, who is last in line?

Read and understand.

What do you know?

There are four friends in all: Liza, Juno, Tessa, and Ashe. There are three clues about their order.

1. Liza is directly in front of Juno.
2. Ashe is directly in front of Tessa.
3. Tessa is somewhere behind Liza.

What are you trying to find?

Which of the four friends is last in line.

Plan.

Let's use the clues and thinking skills.

44

 Solve.

The word "directly" means the friends are right next to each other. There are two sets of friends that are next to each other.

Liza in front of Juno   Ashe in front of Tessa

Tessa is somewhere behind Liza, so Liza and Juno must be in front of Ashe and Tessa.

The order of the friends is:
Liza, Juno, Ashe, Tessa.

The last friend in line is Tessa.

 Look back.

Look back at all of the clues and make sure your answer meets the clues. Is Liza directly in front of Juno? Yes. *Is Ashe directly in front of Tessa?* Yes. *Is Tessa somewhere behind Liza?* Yes.

Let's Review

To solve a word problem, follow these steps:

Read and understand the problem.
Know what the problem says, and what you need to find. If you don't understand, ask questions before you start.

Make a plan.
Choose the plan that makes the most sense and is easiest for you. Remember, there is usually more than one way to find the right answer.

Solve the problem.
Use the plan. If your first plan isn't working, try a different one. Take a break and come back with a fresh mind.

Look back.
Read the problem again. Make sure your answer makes sense. Check your math. If the answer does not look right, don't give up now! Use what you've learned to go back and try the problem again.

Further Reading

Adler, David A. *You Can, Toucan, Math: Word Problem–Solving Fun.* New York: Holiday House, 2006.

Lee, Cora. *The Great Number Rumble: A Story of Math in Surprising Places.* Buffalo, New York: Firefly Books, Inc., 2007.

Scieszka, Jon. *Math Curse.* New York: Viking, 2007.

Tang, Greg. *Math Potatoes: Mind-Stretching Brain Food.* New York: Scholastic Press, 2005.

Internet Addresses

Aplusmath.
  <http://www.aplusmath.com>

Coolmath Games.
  <http://www.coolmath-games.com>

Math Playground.
  <http://www.mathplayground.com/
    wordproblems.html>

Index